The Walking W

Building Your Church

Using Your Gifts, Time, and Resources

Don Cousins & Judson Poling

with contributions from

Bruce Bugbee & Bill Hybels

ZondervanPublishingHouse

Grand Rapids, Michigan

A Division of HarperCollins*Publishers*

The Walking With God Series

Friendship With God:
Developing Intimacy With God

The Incomparable Jesus:
Experiencing the Power of Christ

"Follow Me!":
Walking With Jesus in Everyday Life

Discovering the Church:
Becoming Part of God's New Community

Building Your Church:
Using Your Gifts, Time, and Resources

Impacting Your World:
Becoming a Person of Influence

Published by Zondervan Publishing House, Grand Rapids, Michigan 49530
Produced by The Livingstone Corporation. James C. Galvin, J. Michael Kendrick, Daryl J. Lucas, and Darcy J. Kamps, project staff.

ISBN 0-310-59183-X

Cover design: Mark Veldheer
Interior design: Catherine Bergstrom

Printed in the United States of America
95 96 97 98 99 / DP / 9 8 7 6

Preface

The *Walking With God Series* was developed as the curriculum for small groups at Willow Creek Community Church in South Barrington, Illinois. This innovative church has grown to over 15,000 in less than two decades, and the material here flows out of the vision and values of this dynamic ministry. Groups using these studies have produced many of the leaders, both staff and volunteer, throughout the church.

Associate Pastor Don Cousins wrote the first draft of this material and used it with his own small group. After testing it there, he revised it and passed his notes to Judson Poling, Director of Curriculum Development, who edited and expanded the outlines. Several pilot groups helped shape the material as it was being written and revised. A team of leaders labored through a line-by-line revision of these study guides over a year's span of time. Finally, these revisions were put into this new, more usable format.

Any church or group can use these studies in a relational context to help raise up devoted disciples. Group members who finish all six books will lay a solid foundation for a lifelong walk with God.

Willow Creek Resources is a publishing partnership between Zondervan Publishing House and the Willow Creek Association. Willow Creek Resources will include drama sketches, small group curricula, training material, videos, and many other specialized ministry resources.

Willow Creek Association is an international network of churches ministering to the unchurched. Founded in 1992, the Willow Creek Association serves churches through conferences, seminars, regional roundtables, consulting, and ministry resource materials. The mission of the Association is to assist churches in reestablishing the priority and practice of reaching lost people for Christ through church ministries targeted to seekers.

For conference and seminar information please write to:

Willow Creek Association
P.O. Box 3188
Barrington, Illinois 60011-3188

Contents

Building Your Church

Using Your Gifts, Time, and Resources

Introduction 11

1. Serving: Your Attitude is Everything! 13
2. What Are Spiritual Gifts? 19
3. Primary Spiritual Gifts 23
4. Complementary Spiritual Gifts 35
5. Discovering Your Niche 43
6. Money: Your Attitude is Still Everything! 51
7. Money Matters 57
8. A Foundation for Giving 61
9. Guidelines for Giving 65
10. Motives Matter 71
11. Lessons from Seven Churches (Part 1) 75
12. Lessons from Seven Churches (Part 2) 81
13. Reviewing *Building Your Church* 87

Building Your Church

Using Your Gifts, Time, and Resources

Introduction

What do you feel at the thought of being "used"?

For many people, the term "used" is synonymous with "abused." To be used means having someone else's agenda forced on you. It means being involved in an activity that you don't want to do, which leaves you feeling hollow and unfulfilled. It means giving to the point of exhaustion for the sake of something futile. If that's what it feels like to be "used by God," no wonder some of us can't get very excited about playing our part in the church!

But others see a different picture when they think of God using them. They see a caring heavenly Father who hand-crafted them with special talents and abilities, who longs for them to unfold according to his design. They know he created them with a plan in mind, and he wants them to flourish. They see themselves as givers as well as those who receive help. In serving, they experience more personal growth and greater impact than they'd ever dreamed–all because "God is using them." You can understand how such a vision would inspire these people to be involved in building their church for a lifetime.

One picture leaves us breathless with anticipation–the other, simply out of breath! How can we be sure we increase our service according to the right understanding? God longs to give you living water for service–not so you feel "tapped out," but to help you feel "pumped up." In giving, he wants you to receive. This study, *Building Your Church,* is designed to help you to see how God made you and gifted you, not so he could merely "employ" you, but so you'd experience the joy of being a co-builder of his eternal kingdom. That perspective can help you be a player in his work for the long haul. When your church is full of people with a similar understanding, you will be a collective presence to be reckoned with. God will receive great glory.

And you will never be the same.

Serving: Your Attitude Is Everything

PURPOSE

It's not enough to merely be an attender or even an official member of a local church. We need to be involved. Active service means being more than a spectator. God has accorded us the opportunity to be "players" by giving us spiritual gifts and material resources to make this contribution. Through our service, God fills us with a sense of accomplishment. When we contribute, we find fulfillment.

The purpose of *Building Your Church* is to help us delve further into the ways in which we can contribute to the body of Christ. We will explore the following questions: What should a believer's attitude be toward service? What are spiritual gifts? How do they help the church work in harmony for the benefit of all? How should Christians treat their material possessions? What part of a believer's income should go toward the work of the church? But before we move into a look at the spiritual gifts and the biblical teaching concerning our money and possessions, we need to affirm the *call to serve.*

Our Attitude Toward Service

How would you summarize the key thoughts from Philippians 2:1-4 in your own words?

What are some tangible ways in which we develop those attitudes in our lives? Be specific.

What prevents us from looking to the interests of others with the same attention we devote to ourselves? (Philippians 2:3-4)

What does it mean that we are to have the same attitude as that of Jesus? (Philippians 2:5)

What do you think could help you have more of the same attitude Christ had? Be specific.

What one word do you think best describes the attitude spoken of and modeled by Christ? (Philippians 2:1-11)

God's Call to Service

How does Jesus challenge our customary ideas of how to attain greatness? (Matthew 20:25-28)

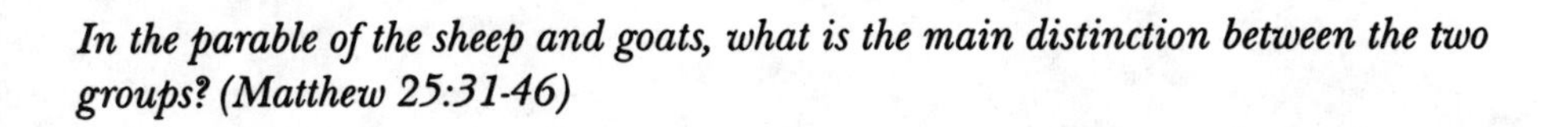

In the parable of the sheep and goats, what is the main distinction between the two groups? (Matthew 25:31-46)

How did members of the early church serve each other? (Acts 2:42-47)

How do people in the church today serve each other?

In what way are we God's workmanship? (Ephesians 2:10)

In what ways could we be serving Christ in our daily activities? (Colossians 3:23-24)

Describe in your own words the benefit of diligent service. (Hebrews 6:10-12)

For what purpose are we to use the gifts we have received? (1 Peter 4:10)

What problem with or attitude toward serving would you like God to change in you?

Bottom Line

Your Walk with God

Bible

Read and study 1 Corinthians 12:1-31 at least three times this week.

Prayer

Day One: In what ways has God been patient with you? In what ways has he demonstrated faithfulness to you even when you were unfaithful toward him? Express your thankfulness to God for his kindness.

Day Two: Reflect back over the events, conversations, thoughts, and deeds of the past few days. For what do you need to claim God's forgiveness?

Day Three: Make a list of the material blessings for which you can thank God. Then read James 1:16-17. In light of your list, what is the significance of those verses?

Scripture Memory

As part of the curriculum, we've included memory verses with each study. If you desire to make this discipline part of your discipleship experience, begin by memorizing this verse:

Follow the way of love and eagerly desire spiritual gifts. 1 Corinthians 14:1

The next study will be the first of four on the topic of spiritual gifts. Before the next meeting, think of how you would describe a spiritual gift to a new believer.

2

What Are Spiritual Gifts?

Purpose

The Holy Spirit has given every believer unique gifts that are to be used to accomplish God's purposes. Everyone can feel a part of the grand design when he or she employs these gifts in the way God intended. So what's your gift?

Finding your niche is as simple as understanding what the Bible says about gifts, then discovering and using these gifts in your church. It is exciting to learn that spiritual gifts are given to every Christian, but it's sobering to learn how greatly God depends on us to use our gifts wisely to accomplish his work. Still, many believers have only a murky understanding about spiritual gifts and how they relate to the work of the church. In this study you will learn more about how God intended spiritual gifts to work in the body of Christ.

Study

How would you describe spiritual gifts to a new Christian?

What does Paul wish for believers regarding spiritual gifts? (1 Corinthians 12:1)

How do we decide what spiritual gift we will receive? (1 Corinthians 12:4-6, 11)

Why does God give us spiritual gifts? (1 Corinthians 12:7)

How should our spiritual gifts interact with each other? (1 Corinthians 12:12-20)

What do you think are the reasons why churches don't experience a more harmonious interaction of spiritual gifts?

Why would the goal of spiritual maturity not be to obtain as many gifts as possible? (1 Corinthians 12:28-30)

Why would God see to it that everyone has at least one gift?

Based on 1 Corinthians 12:1-30, what conclusions can you draw about how the gifts are supposed to function in the church?

How would you relate the Parable of the Talents to our use of spiritual gifts? (Matthew 25:14-30)

How would you describe the kind of church that results when people discover and use their spiritual gifts? (Ephesians 4:7-16)

What must be added to our gifts to make them beneficial to the giver and the recipient? (1 Corinthians 13:1-3)

Why do you suppose that Paul had to include this instruction to the Corinthian church?

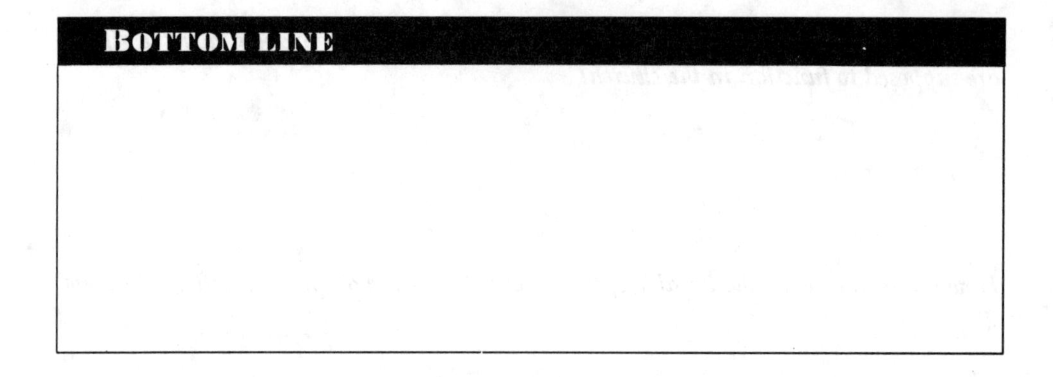

YOUR WALK WITH GOD

Bible

Read Romans 12:1-21, noting observations and applications.

Prayer

Day One: Pray that God will grant you discernment in the days and weeks ahead to discover your gifts and use them in the most effective manner for serving the church.

Day Two: Pray for three areas of character that you need God to strengthen.

Day Three: Pray specifically for ten people in your life who need your prayer for their needs.

Scripture Memory

Serve wholeheartedly, as if you were serving the Lord, not men. Ephesians 6:7

Next time we will look more closely at the most important gifts God has provided for the church. To prepare, ask yourself: What gifts do individuals in your church possess that are particularly important to the well-being of the body?

Primary Spiritual Gifts

Purpose

Imagine a family with a permanent Christmas tree in their house. Under that tree sits a pile of presents—each one purchased with love and thoughtfulness, then carefully wrapped and put under the tree. Yet it would be a shame if the presents remained there, beautifully wrapped but never enjoyed as the packages of love they were intended to be. The receivers would never experience the gifts, the givers would never be appreciated for giving the gift, and the family would never benefit from the use of the gift.

Your church was not designed to be a house full of unwrapped gifts. When all members know the gifts God has given them and use them for the common good, everybody wins—the receiver becomes fruitful and fulfilled, the body receives the ministry God intended, and God is glorified whenever the church operates according to his design. This study will help you understand a simple classification of gifts, and then help your group grasp how primary gifts are to be used in the church.

Study

One outline of spiritual gifts divides them into two broad categories: *Primary* gifts and *complementary* gifts. The primary gifts can be further subdivided into speaking, service, and relational gifts. The following chart shows this breakdown:

PRIMARY GIFTS

Speaking Gifts

- Prophecy
- Teaching

Service Gifts

- Administration
- Helps
- Giving

Relational Gifts

- Encouragement
- Evangelism
- Hospitality
- Leadership
- Mercy
- Shepherding

COMPLEMENTARY GIFTS

- Apostleship
- Discernment
- Faith
- Healing
- Interpretation
- Knowledge
- Miracles
- Tongues
- Wisdom

ADDITIONAL GIFTS

- Craftsmanship
- Creative Communication

Now that we have the big picture, let's look at the gifts in detail:

Prophecy

Why do you think Paul placed prophecy in such high esteem? (1 Corinthians 14:1-5, 24-25)

What potential problem could someone who has the gift of prophecy develop? (2 Corinthians 12:7-10)

Teaching

What is the gift of teaching? (Ephesians 4:11)

What warning does James give those who want to be teachers? (James 3:1)

What role do the speaking gifts play in the life of the church?

Administration

Why was the gift of administration so vital to the ministry of the early church? (Acts 6:1-4)

Why is the gift of administration still needed in churches today?

Giving

If all Christians are supposed to give financially to their church, why would giving be singled out as a spiritual gift?

What would you say are the differences between those who give to God's work (which is all of us) and those who have the gift of giving?

Helps

How did Epaphroditus exhibit the gift of helps? (Philippians 2:25-30).

Encouragement

Why is encouragement a valuable gift in the church?

Evangelism

How did Philip exhibit the gift of evangelism? (Acts 8:26-40)

How would you describe the difference between the gift of evangelism and the responsibility all believers have for evangelism?

Hospitality

What can we learn from Lydia's example about hospitality to other Christians? (Acts 16:14-15)

Leadership

What are the main obligations of those with the gift of leadership? (Hebrews 13:17)

Mercy

In what ministries of the church would the gift of mercy be especially valuable?

Shepherding

Most people associate this gift with the senior pastor of a church. How might God use this gift in other ministries of the church?

BOTTOM LINE

YOUR WALK WITH GOD

Bible

Study 1 Corinthians 13:1-13, noting observations and applications.

Prayer

Day One: After reading 1 Corinthians 13, jot down all the characteristics of love listed, in verses 4 through 8. Then write down next to each characteristic one way in which God has demonstrated that characteristic to you.

Day Two: Looking back over the past week, in what ways have you failed to demonstrate the love described in 1 Corinthians 13?

Day Three: Make a list of people who have demonstrated genuine love in one form or another toward you, listing next to each person's name how that love was expressed. Thank God for them.

Scripture Memory

Now to each one the manifestation of the Spirit is given for the common good.
1 Corinthians 12:7

The next study will examine the complementary gifts–those attributes that support and enhance the primary gifts. To prepare, think of a time when you played an important supporting role in someone else's work. What gifts did you bring to the job that contributed to the success of the effort?

ON YOUR OWN

For next week, fill out the questionnaire below to help you identify what your spiritual gifts are.

Character Trait Assessment

This Character Trait Assessment has been designed to assist you in the identification of your primary gift(s). There are certain character qualities that often correspond to the manifestation of specific gifts in one's life.

Place a check by those statements than are true and best describe you or your tendencies most of the time. Total the number of items checked in each section.

Section A

___ More expressive/dominant than submissive/tolerant/inhibited

___ Feels responsible to confront people with truth

___ Strongly opinionated and individualistic

___ Able to apply biblical truths to everyday situations

___ Willing to experience brokenness to encourage brokenness in others

___ Messages bring conviction and change in the lives of others

___ More depressed than light-hearted about life and its problems

___ SECTION A TOTAL

Section B

___ More composed/tolerant/empathetic than nervous/hostile

___ Willing to spend much time caring/nurturing a group of people

___ Desires and has needs for intimate spiritual relationships

___ Tendency to compromise rather than go to either extreme

___ Compelled to lead by example and model

___ Spiritually develops others patiently and responsibly

___ Willing to renounce personal interests for the sake of others

___ SECTION B TOTAL

Section C

___ Thorough and careful, skilled in details

___ More composed than nervous, more objective than subjective

___ Able to see the overall picture and anticipate possible implications

___ Clarifies goals and develops strategies to accomplish them

___ Feels frustration and sadness at disorganization

___ Able to identify and effectively use resources to accomplish tasks

___ Concerned for the productivity of kingdom work more than personal desires

___ SECTION C TOTAL

Section D

___ Likes people and relates well

___ Strong desire to share their faith with unbelievers

___ Discerns spiritual needs in others

___ More sympathetic/subjective than indifferent/objective

___ Communicates the gospel with clarity, poise, and effectiveness

___ Committed to placing new converts in the body of Christ

___ Enjoys building relationships with unchurched people

___ SECTION D TOTAL

Section E

___ Conscientious person

___ Desires to give quietly without public notice, yet needs to feel liked

___ Gives gifts of enduring value

___ Wrestles with being faithful in issues of money management

___ Able to give liberally and joyfully

___ Desires to use their giving as a way to motivate others to give

___ Feels a part of the work to which they give

___ SECTION E TOTAL

Section F

___ Genuinely enjoys providing a place for others in need

___ Appreciates every guest the Lord brings into their home

___ Concerned with meeting a need, not making an impression

___ Tends to be easygoing and feels comfortable around strangers

___ Fulfilled by serving people who cannot pay them back

___ Enjoys all classes of people and feels at ease with them

___ New people in the church migrate to you

___ SECTION F TOTAL

Section G

___ Friends seem to wait on your decisions

___ Able to motivate others toward a goal

___ Consciously sets an example for others

___ Influences others to be all God wants them to be

___ Confident, practical, applies common sense

___ Feels alone in making certain decisions

___ Able to live with disagreement

___ SECTION G TOTAL

Section H

___ Tendency toward a low self-image

___ Others easily confide in you

___ Strong desires to remove the causes of people's hurts

___ Very empathetic, patient, tolerant, and impulsive

___ Able to express love in tangible ways

___ Reacts harshly when people are hurt, displaced, or rejected

___ A positive faith that does not become easily depressed

___ SECTION H TOTAL

Section I

___ Identifies needs and desires to help meet them personally

___ Usually easygoing, loyal, wants to be liked

___ Enjoys serving when it frees others to better accomplish their ministry

___ Publicly more inhibited than expressive

___ Has trouble saying no, which often results in overinvolvement

___ Tendency to feel inadequate and unqualified for spiritual leadership

___ Likes short-range projects better than long-range responsibilities

___ SECTION I TOTAL

Section J

___ Studies, understands, and shares truth from God's Word

___ More objective/self-disciplined than subjective/spontaneous

___ Gathers truth and presents it in an organized manner

___ Listens with a discerning ear to the teaching of others

___ Analytical, makes decisions based on facts

___ Enjoys researching an idea and effectively communicating it to others at their level

___ Able to stimulate others to understand truth and obey it

___ SECTION J TOTAL

Section K

___ More tolerant/sympathetic than hostile/indifferent

___ Tends to be positive and full of faith

___ Strong desire to see people fully mature spiritually

___ Enjoys strengthening the weak and reassuring the unstable

___ Views trials as divine opportunities for growth

___ Likes to challenge and is willing to rebuke to cause growth in others

___ Spontaneously discerns needs and encourages individually those in the trenches

___ SECTION K TOTAL

List, in order, the letters of the sections with the four highest scores (highest to lowest). Write in the corresponding gift.

	Score	Section Letter	Gift
1			
2			
3			
4			

Key
A. Prophecy
B. Shepherding
C. Administration
D. Evangelism
E. Giving
F. Hospitality
G. Leadership
H. Mercy
I. Helps
J. Teaching
K. Encouragement

Complementary Spiritual Gifts

Purpose

The church is many separate individuals but at the same time one body. Spiritual gifts help us work together with other believers so that the church can function as one. Our gifts also distinguish us as valuable participants who can make a unique contribution to the life the church. Unfortunately, sometimes the gifts divide the body of Christ. People become proud of the gifts they possess and feel smug in their spiritual status. Others don't value some of the gifts and cut themselves off from the benefits that would come if everyone were allowed to make his or her contribution. Still others attribute undue importance to gifts that should be exercised in a support role.

Paul wisely nestled the famous love chapter of 1 Corinthians 13 in the middle of his discussion on spiritual gifts so that we'd be reminded of what the use of spiritual gifts is supposed to produce. With love as the goal, we can employ our gift and be "one" and "many" at the same time. This study will help you understand the purpose of the complementary gifts and how they should be exercised properly within the church.

Study

The last study covered the primary spiritual gifts: encouragement, evangelism, hospitality, leadership, mercy, shepherding, prophecy, teaching, administration, helps, and giving. Now we move on to cover the complementary gifts. They are called complementary because they are designed to enhance the primary gifts. They do not function in isolation or assume the importance of a primary gift, either for the individual or for the church. Problems sometimes develop in a church when complementary gifts are elevated above the primary gifts. Complementary gifts serve best when they undergird and enhance the operation of the other gifts.

Apostleship

What does a person with the gift of apostleship do? (Acts 1:23-26)

What problems might arise if someone tried to start a church without also having the gift of leadership and administration?

Discernment

What harm might come to a church if people with discernment neglect to use their gift?

Faith

What is the difference between the faith we all possess and the gift of faith? (1 Corinthians 12:9)

Healing

In what ways might God give someone the gift of healing other than the sudden, dramatic gifts displayed by Peter (Acts 3:6-7) and Paul (Acts 28:8-9)?

Miracles

What special temptations or problems would a person entrusted with the gift of miracles face?

Knowledge

Why is the gift of knowledge valuable for every church?

Wisdom

How would you describe the difference between knowledge and wisdom?

Tongues

Why does Paul regard other gifts as more important than the gift of tongues? (1 Corinthians 12:28; 14:2-5)

Interpretation

What special instructions does Paul give for the gift of interpretation? (1 Corinthians 14:11-12, 19, 26-28)

Additional Gifts

We place any other spiritual gifts not specifically mentioned above in this category. These gifts also make valuable contributions to the body of Christ. This list is not exhaustive–you may have other gifts you want to include.

Craftsmanship

How might the gift of craftsmanship be put to use for the church?

Creative Communication

What might this gift provide for a church?

Conclusion

How can we promote a healthier understanding and use of spiritual gifts in our church?

Bottom Line

YOUR WALK WITH GOD

Bible

Read 2 Corinthians 5:1-21 during your three appointments with God.

Prayer

Day One: Pray for specific ways you can learn to live by faith, not sight (2 Corinthians 5:7).

Day Two: Pray that you can make it your goal to please the Lord whatever your personal circumstances (2 Corinthians 5:9).

Day Three: Pray for three people for whom you are trying to be an effective ambassador for Christ (2 Corinthians 5:20).

Scripture Memory

Review 1 Corinthians 14:1, Ephesians 6:7, and 1 Corinthians 12:7 for next week.

Having looked at spiritual gifts and the ways in which you can determine yours, next time we will examine ways of making sure you are working in a ministry that is suited to your particular gift.

ON YOUR OWN

Observation Assessment

Instructions

1. Make two copies of the Observation Assessment found on the following pages.

2. Identify two people who know you well. Preferably, they should be Christians who have observed you in a ministry. If not, they should at least be people likely to have an accurate perception of you. (If you want more than two people to evaluate you, make additional copies of the assessments.)

3. Ask these people to read each gift description carefully and comment appropriately. Their thoughtful reflections will assist you in understanding who God made you to be. Ask them to return the assessment to you within a week.

4. Remember that people's perceptions will be affected by how long they have known you and the type of relationship they have with you (family, small group, work, and so on). Weigh these factors as you evaluate and record their responses.

5. Study the observations you receive and determine which gifts seem to be most affirmed.

Observation Assessment Form

Observations of ________________ Completed by ________________

Your friend or family member is seeking to better understand who God has made him or her to be. Your perspective and observations can be helpful in that process. Thank you for your time in completing this questionnaire.

Directions: Read each of the descriptions below. Using these definitions, mark one of the following letters in the each of the spaces provided.

Y = Yes, definitely true, certain gift

P = Perhaps, possibly true, potential gift

N = No, does not have this gift

? = I don't know, have not observed this

___ **ADMINSTRATION:** The divine enablement to understand what make an organization function, and the special ability to plan and execute procedures that increase the church's organizational effectiveness.

___ **COUNSELING:** The divine enablement to effectively listen to people and assist them in their quest for wholeness.

___ **CRAFTSMANSHIP:** The divine enablement to facilitate ministry through the creative construction of necessary tools for ministry.

___ **CREATIVE COMMUNICATION:** The divine enablement to communicate God's truth through a variety of art forms.

___ **ENCOURAGEMENT:** The divine enablement to reassure, strengthen, and affirm those who are discouraged or wavering in their faith.

___ **EVANGELISM:** The divine enablement to effectively communicate the message of Christ to unbelievers so they can respond in faith and discipleship.

___ **GIVING:** The divine enablement to contribute money and material resources to the work of the Lord with cheerfulness and generosity.

___ **HELPS:** The divine enablement to accomplish practical and necessary tasks that support the body of Christ.

___ **HOSPITALITY:** The divine enablement to care for people by providing fellowship, food, and shelter.

___ **LEADERSHIP:** The divine enablement to instill vision, to motivate, and to direct people to accomplish the work of the ministry.

___ **MERCY:** The divine enablement to minister cheerfully and appropriately to people who are suffering.

___ **PROPHECY:** The divine enablement to proclaim God's truth with power and clarity in a timely and culturally sensitive fashion for correction, repentance, or encouragement.

___ **SHEPHERDING:** The divine enablement to guide, care for, and nurture individuals or groups in the body as they grow in their faith.

___ **TEACHING:** The divine enablement to understand, clearly explain, and apply the Word of God to the lives of listeners.

a. Do you have any other observations or insights that would help this person to understand his or her strengths or abilities?

____

____

b. Look back at those gifts you marked "Y" (definitely true). List them from most apparent to least apparent and explain why you think this person has these gifts.

1. GIFT ________________________ WHY?________________________

2. GIFT ________________________ WHY?________________________

3. GIFT ________________________ WHY?________________________

c. List in order the two top gifts you marked with a "P" (possibly true) and explain why you believe the person might have those gifts.

1. GIFT ________________________ WHY?________________________

2. GIFT ________________________ WHY?________________________

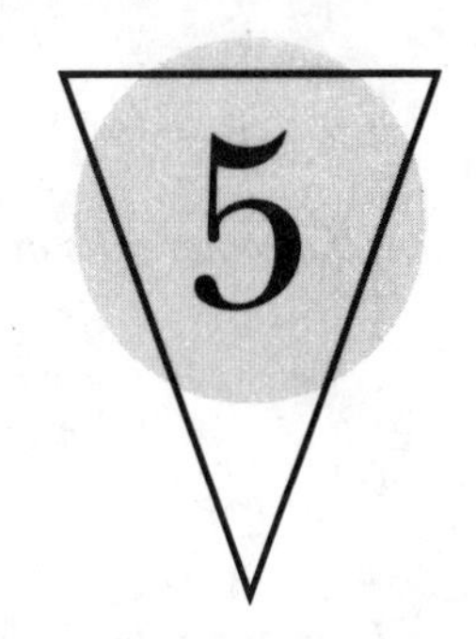

Discovering Your Niche

PURPOSE

Does it make a difference which ministry you volunteer for? Have you ever felt resentful because you were working in a ministry that you didn't particularly enjoy, yet had to be done? Have you ever wondered what God is calling you to do?

Doing the right thing and having God's approval is important to ministry, but so is ministering in the right place. While many "soldiers of grace" are to be commended for diligently working without recognition and without reward, some people stay in the wrong place out of a misguided sense of duty. Involved people sometimes get the idea that the less they like their service, the more God must be pleased with it. God may well have something better for them that is more in keeping with their gifts, talents, and abilities. He teaches us in his Word that we all have different gifts so our uniqueness can be celebrated, and so ministry can be both effective and personally fulfilling. Discovering our gifts is the first step toward fulfilling God's plan for us; finding our niche is the next.

STUDY

Identifying Your Gift

What is your primary gift?

What other gifts or abilities have been affirmed by others who know you?

How accurate do you feel these assessments of your gifts are?

Developing Your Gift

Describe in your own words the principle taught in Matthew 25:19-21. How might this idea be applied to spiritual gifts?

Read Acts 18:24-28. What do you see in this story about the development of spiritual gifts?

What are some ways you could develop your spiritual gifts? Be specific.

Misuse of Gifts

How might gifts be misused?

Projection–Expecting other Christians to possess our spiritual gifts and to serve as effectively as we do in similar situations.

Status Seeking–Holding our gifts as more important than other people's gifts and seeking special status for ourselves among other believers.

Isolation–Using our spiritual gifts for personal satisfaction or gain rather than for the common good (1 Corinthians 12:7).

Suppression–Suppressing the expression of our spiritual gifts because we doubt their validity, importance, or impact (1 Timothy 4:14).

Arrogance–Taking credit for the results of our gifts instead of giving the glory to God (Proverbs 25:14).

Which of the above abuses do you need to be alert to in particular?

Other hindrances can affect the fruitfulness of our ministries. As you look at the table below, what areas of weakness do you think could affect the use of your gift?

The Presence of . . .	The Lack of . . .
Sin	Development
False Humility	Love
Pride	Availability

Gifts and Passions

In addition to spiritual gifts, we all have strong desires and interests that God uses to direct us into an area of service that fits us best. Take a few moments to answer the questions below relating to your passion or particular interest.

I prefer to work with:

___ things　　___ information

___ people　　___ other __________

I am attracted to and have the greatest concern for:

___ infants　　___ children

___ teens　　___ young adults

___ adults　　___ singles

___ couples ___ the elderly

___ other __________

My deepest desire is to make a difference in the following area:

___ global concerns ___ politics

___ secular society ___ economics

___ church ___ other ____________

I think the greatest need I could address is:

If money, time, family, or education were not an issue, and if I knew I could not fail, I would do the following:

If I could make a difference and impact an area of ministry, I would do the following:

Based upon my responses, the two areas that I have a passion for are:

Am I in the Right Place?

Sometimes a problem in the church is when people are willing to serve and are even faithful in their service but don't feel fruitful or fulfilled. If you're one of those people, you might be asking yourself, *Am I in the right place?*

In Acts 6:1-4, the twelve apostles realized they were performing tasks that weren't particularly suited to their gifts. What was the situation?

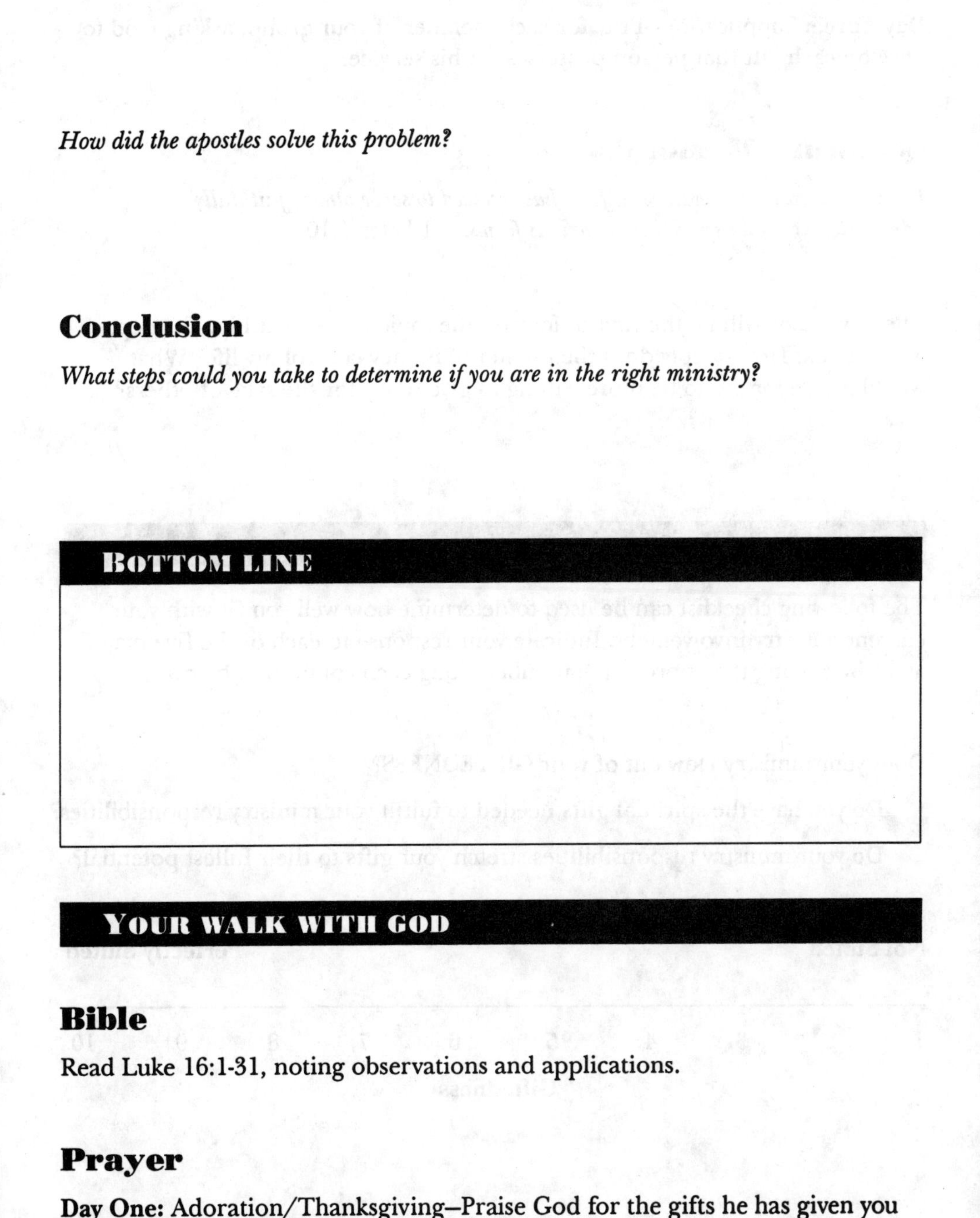

What were some of the frustrations and problems developing in this situation?

How did the apostles solve this problem?

Conclusion

What steps could you take to determine if you are in the right ministry?

BOTTOM LINE

YOUR WALK WITH GOD

Bible

Read Luke 16:1-31, noting observations and applications.

Prayer

Day One: Adoration/Thanksgiving–Praise God for the gifts he has given you and the members of your group.

Day Two: Confession—Examine yourself and confess times when you've misused or neglected spiritual gifts.

Day Three: Supplication—Pray for each member of your group, asking God to develop each gift that person possesses for his service.

Scripture Memory

Each one should use whatever gift he has received to serve others, faithfully administering God's grace in its various forms. 1 Peter 4:10

The next study will be the first of four on the topic of stewardship. To prepare, ask yourself: How deeply does the pursuit of money control my life? What would it take for me to be more willing to give freely for the sake of others?

On Your Own

The following checklist can be used to determine how well you fit with your current ministry involvement. Indicate your response to each of the five major areas by circling the appropriate number along each continuum below.

Does your ministry flow out of your GIFTEDNESS?

Do you have the spiritual gifts needed to fulfill your ministry responsibilities?

Do your ministry responsibilities stretch your gifts to their fullest potential?

Not Suited **Perfectly Suited**

1 2 3 4 5 6 7 8 9 10

Giftedness

Does your ministry reflect your PASSION?

What need is of ultimate importance to you?

Does your ministry in some way address this need?

Not Suited									**Perfectly Suited**
1	2	3	4	5	6	7	8	9	10

Passion

Are you receiving RELATIONAL affirmation?

Do your co-workers within the ministry verbally affirm your contribution? Does leadership? Or is there a curious silence from these people about your service?

Not Suited									**Perfectly Suited**
1	2	3	4	5	6	7	8	9	10

Relational Affirmation

Are you receiving MINISTRY affirmation?

Are you being fruitful? Can you see results?

Are those you are serving being encouraged and challenged?

Not Suited									**Perfectly Suited**
1	2	3	4	5	6	7	8	9	10

Ministry Affirmation

Are you receiving PERSONAL affirmation?

Are you being fulfilled?

Do your feel better about yourself after serving this ministry?

Is your self-esteem healthier?

Not Suited									**Perfectly Suited**
1	2	3	4	5	6	7	8	9	10

Personal Affirmation

Total the five numbers you circled:

45–50	Serving properly.
38–44	Probably in the right ministry (but you may need more serving experience).
30–37	Some minor changes in where you serve may make you more effective.
0–30	Seek counsel with your church leaders regarding a ministry more in line with who God made you to be.

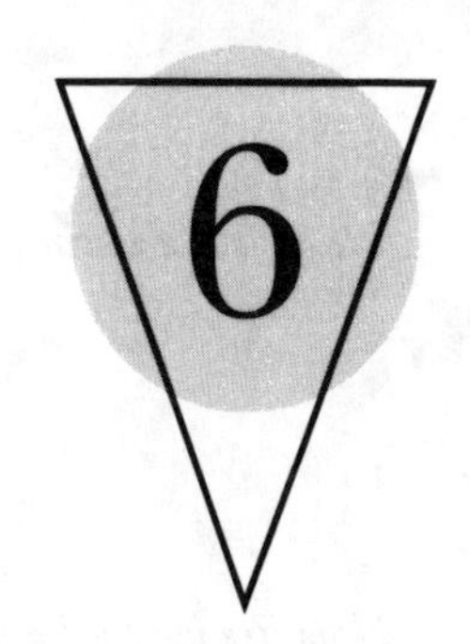

Money: Your Attitude Is Still Everything

PURPOSE

The story of the rich young ruler is one of the saddest in the New Testament because here we see someone who wants to love God above everything, but money gets in the way. Instead of repenting, he decides to walk away.

We may actually have more in common with the rich young man than we're comfortable admitting. We too may think we're open to Christ, impressed with who he is, and ready to respond to what he may demand of us. But when we find out what he demands of us and discover that he is Lord of everything, including our checkbooks and credit cards, our readiness may give way to regret. Our craving for righteousness may not be as strong as our appetite for money. The "things we are going to do for God" once our lives become manageable may be buried along with our overworked and prematurely deceased bodies.

STUDY

The Rich Fool

What circumstance led Jesus to tell the parable about the rich man? (Luke 12:13-15)

What is the main point of the parable? (Luke 12:16-21)

How are we challenged to reorder our priorities toward possessions? (Luke 12:22-34)

The Rich Young Ruler

Which of the Ten Commandments had the rich young ruler failed to obey? (Luke 18:18-30)

Why is it so hard for the rich to enter the Kingdom of Heaven?

How does Jesus respond to the question "Who can be saved?" (Luke 18:27)

What do you see as the main point of the passage?

The Shrewd Manager

Read Luke 16:1-13. Why was the manager in trouble with the rich man?

What was the manager's plan to better his prospects after he left the rich man's employ? (Luke 16:5-7)

How did the boss react to the manager's actions? (Luke 16:8)

How do you understand the advice Jesus gave to the disciples about shrewdness and using wealth? (Luke 16:8-9)

Principles of Christian Stewardship

Note: These principles were originally outlined by Bill Hybels of Willow Creek Community Church.

Be faithful

What can you learn about faithfulness with finances from Luke 16:10?

Use money as a training ground

Why would handling money be a test for handling true riches? (Luke 16:11)

Ownership follows stewardship

Why is important is important to be a good steward if you only have a little bit of money? (Luke 16:12)

Serve only one master

Why is personal financial management a true indicator of where your heart is toward God? (Luke 16:13)

What step could you take this week to put one of these four principles into action?

BOTTOM LINE

Bible

Read one of the following passages each day, making observations and applications:

1 Timothy 5:8; 1 Thessalonians 4:11-12; 1 Timothy 6:6-11, 17-19.

Prayer

Day One: Adoration–Look up Hebrews 12:7-11. Can you identify any ways in which God has disciplined you in recent weeks (or months)? Make a list and worship him for being an "involved" heavenly parent.

Day Two: Confession–Quiet your heart and ask God to reveal to you any bitterness, resentment, or hard feelings that you may be holding toward someone. What will it take to see total forgiveness extended? Take a step in that direction this week.

Day Three: Thanksgiving/Supplication–Make a list of material wants that God in his grace has enabled you to taste and enjoy. Pray over your attitude toward money and the material things it can buy. What are you currently "worrying" about financially? What possessions (owned or yet to be obtained) are you "serving"?

Scripture Memory

So if you have not been trustworthy in handling worldly wealth, who will trust you with true riches? Luke 16:11

In the next study we will continue our study of wealth and possessions by looking at more verses that pertain to the subject. Ask yourself: What percentage of my income would I be willing to give away to advance God's work?

Money Matters

Purpose

A tale is told of a man who was down and out, desperate, and with only two dollars left to his name. As he sat in church one day praying, he decided to place his last two dollars in the offering plate, believing that God would honor his faith and bless him in return.

As it turned out, the man walked out of church and immediately stumbled onto a business opportunity that required no initial investment and earned him a fortune within a matter of months. This same now very wealthy gentleman returned to the church where he had made his faith pledge. Before the sermon, he began to tell the man next to him about how he had sat in that very spot just months previously in rags, crying out to God, and then how he deposited his last two dollars in the offering plate. "As a result," he related, "God made me a millionaire." After a moment of reflection the young man sitting next to him responded, "You gave all the money you had to your name?" The gentleman proudly replied, "That's right!" The other man paused again for a moment and then said in a low voice, "I dare you to do it again!"

Generally, it's what we keep that more correctly exposes our attitude in giving. This is why the Scriptures emphasize motives and faith rather than dollar amounts and results. Certainly carelessness and poor stewardship are as bad as stinginess and selfishness. But everyone must examine himself or herself under the light of God's Word with the scrutiny of God's Spirit in order to be sure that both how we give and what we keep are pleasing to God.

Study

Why would a person who did not provide for his immediate family be regarded as worse than an unbeliever? (1 Timothy 5:8)

What specific application could you draw from 1 Timothy 5:8?

What wisdom do you find in Paul's advice that believers lead a "quiet life"? (1 Thessalonians 4:11-12)

How would you characterize the "great gain" Paul describes? (1 Timothy 6:6)

How does Paul's advice to be content with food and clothing contrast to what our society tells us to be content with? (1 Timothy 6:8)

How do you distinguish between you needs and wants?

Why is pursuing riches a trap? (1 Timothy 6:9)

Why is it dangerous to love money? (1 Timothy 6:10)

How could you overcome a tendency to love money too dearly?

What advice does Paul give those who have wealth? (1 Timothy 6:17-18)

What are some ways we can share our material blessings with others?

Conclusion

What can you do this week to bring your finances under the lordship of Christ?

BOTTOM LINE

YOUR WALK WITH GOD

Bible

Spend time each day reading and reflecting on the truths contained in Philippians 3:1-21. What specific, practical applications can you make after meditating on these verses?

Prayer

Day One: Pray for your use of money, that you may be faithful in giving in the quantity and quality God requires of you.

Day Two: Pray for those in your group who are struggling with their management of God's resources.

Day Three: Pray for the financial stewardship of your church's funds, that money would be spent wisely for God's work.

Scripture Memory

Keep your lives free from the love of money and be content with what you have, because God has said, "Never will I leave you; never will I forsake you." Hebrews 13:5

For next week, write a summary of the important points you have gained from lessons 6 and 7. Try to come up with five or six ideas. You will be sharing from these summaries next week.

A Foundation for Giving

PURPOSE

We all know that the Bible gives us very practical advice for living. All of us have turned to its pages for wisdom about family relationships, personal integrity, discipleship, and so on. But what does the Bible have to say about money? When we study the Scriptures, we find a rich lode of sensible advice for handling our financial affairs. From the Book of Genesis through the letters to the New Testament churches, God has outlined a consistent, practical system for good stewardship. The purpose of this study is to expose you to the breadth of God's teaching on money and possessions and to help you apply that wisdom to your own circumstances.

STUDY

What led you to choose the principles you ended up selecting from lessons 6 and 7?

Of the points you listed, which one do you think God would want you to work on first?

What enabled Paul to count everything loss compared to the greatness of knowing Christ? (Philippians 3:8-9)

How does James 2:14-16 speak to your present attitude of sharing with others?

In what practical ways can we help those with genuine needs?

Why should we link true contentment with avoiding love of money? (Hebrews 13:5)

What important principles of giving can be found from the meeting of Abram and Melchizedek? (Genesis 14:14-20)

What similar principles about giving do we find in the Mosaic law? (Leviticus 27:30, 32)

What can we learn about the importance of the tithe from Malachi 3:8-10?

What did Jesus find lacking in the Pharisees' attitude toward tithing? (Matthew 23:23)

What principle about giving can we draw from Jesus' warning to the Pharisees? (Matthew 23:23)

How would you summarize the Bible's perspective on stewardship?

Review the list that you brought to the study. What changes would you want to make to the list based on your discussion in the group?

What can you do this week to begin to make a change for the better?

BOTTOM LINE

Bible

Read 2 Corinthians 8 and 9, noting especially those verses that have to do with giving.

Prayer

You are to pray over the statement you selected during this study. Pray also for the needs of two other people in the group who have voiced concern about their giving and stewardship.

Scripture Memory

Review 1 Peter 4:10, Luke 16:11, and Hebrews 13:5 for next week.

Our next study, based on Paul's second letter to the Corinthians, will contain some practical advice for the way we should help other believers and our church with our material resources.

Guidelines for Giving

Purpose

How does God look at the way we treat our possessions? An everyday comparison might be the way a parent observes and disciplines a young child. When the youngster is generous with his or her playmates, willing to share toys, a book, or snacks, the parent is pleased with the child's behavior. On the other hand, the child who refuses to share grieves the parent. In fact, such selfishness can anger the parent enough that the child is punished. God looks at our use of money in much the same way. When we give gladly and freely, it pleases him. But when we insist that everything we have is at our disposal, our discretion, it grieves the God who has given us everything we have.

This study will show you what you should consider when giving. We'll look at the example of one New Testament church that struggled with the issue. Then we'll summarize the teaching on giving we've learned so far.

Study

Guidelines for Giving

In what ways are you finding your attitude toward giving and managing your possessions changing?

Turn to 2 Corinthians 8:1-5. What do we know about the Macedonian churches that might encourage Christians who are reluctant to give because they have few resources?

What had apparently happened the original commitment made by the Corinthians? (2 Corinthians 8:6-15)

What important principles of giving does Paul teach in this letter? (2 Corinthians 8:6-15)

What did Paul do to spur the Corinthians to action? (2 Corinthians 8:16–9:5)

What kind of a letter would Paul write to you about your follow-through on financial commitments to other Christians?

Why is how much we give related to how much we will receive in return? (2 Corinthians 9:6)

Why is it important that we give "not reluctantly or under compulsion"? (2 Corinthians 9:7)

What is a "cheerful" giver? (2 Corinthians 9:7)

How does God reward faithful giving? (2 Corinthians 9:8)

Why does Paul sum up his discussion on giving with an expression of thanks? (2 Corinthians 9:15)

Summary on Giving

Which of the following key principles from the New Testament is most difficult for you to swallow? Why?

All that I have belongs to the Lord.

Keep only what I need to meet my needs.

Give the remainder to God's work.

How should you decide how much to give to God's work?

To whom should you give your contribution?

What is the next step you should take to make this study a reality to you and your family?

BOTTOM LINE

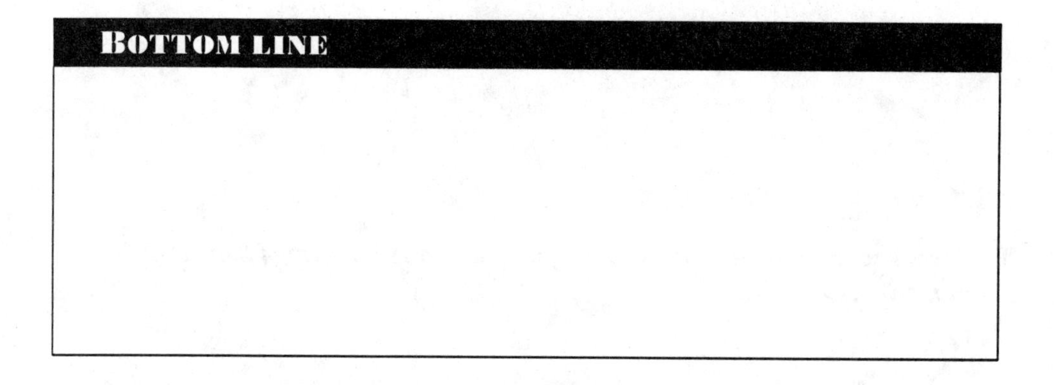

YOUR WALK WITH GOD

Bible

Read Matthew 6:1-8, noting observations and applications.

Prayer

Day One: Reflect on how God has manifested his kindness to you. Spend time in prayer adoring his wonderful character.

Day Two: What have you found yourself complaining about recently? How have you violated Paul's command to "do everything without complaining or arguing" (Philippians 2:14)? Confess any sin in this area.

Day Three: Pray for yourself in regards to how you can be more of a contributing member of the church. Ask God to help you be a *relational* contributor, a *serving* contributor, and a *giving* contributor.

Scripture Memory

Each man should give what he has decided in his heart to give, not reluctantly or under compulsion, for God loves a cheerful giver. 2 Corinthians 9:7

Our motives for serving others will be the topic of the next study. To prepare, ask yourself: If I knew nobody was aware of the work I did for my church, would it affect at all the way I served?

On Your Own

Read the following essay for the next meeting.

Christian Giving

by Dr. Gilbert Bilezikian

It is generally recognized that, according to the Old Testament, the tenth of one's income represented a required minimum amount of giving to God's work by the people of the old covenant.

The New Testament reverses this principle. It requires new covenant believers to regard all of their income as belonging to God–not just the tithe (Matthew 6:19-34; 19:16-30; Luke 9:23-25; 12:13-34; 16:1-13; 18:18-30; 21:1-4; Acts 2:44-45; 4:32-37).

The New Testament enjoins Christians to keep for themselves only that which is necessary to provide for them and their dependents so that they do not become a burden on others (1 Thessalonians 4:11-12; 1 Timothy 5:8; 6:6-10).

Consequently, the portion of their wealth that exceeds what is necessary for their needs is to be used for God's work and for deeds of charity (2 Corinthians 9:6-15; Galatians 6:10; 1 Timothy 6:17-19; James 2:15-16; 1 John 3:16-18).

Thus, whereas the Old Testament required the contribution of only a tenth of one's income to God's work, the New Testament requires the total disposition of one's possessions for God, except the portion which is to be kept for oneself and one's relatives. On this basis, if the tenth of one's income is sufficient to provide for one's own and family needs, the remaining ninety percent belongs to God's work.

Old covenant believers were to set aside a tenth of their income for God. New covenant believers are to set aside for themselves only that which is required for their needs. The remainder belongs to God and is to be rendered to Him as an expression of worship.

This reversal of the old covenant standard provides an explanation for the New Testament's relative silence on the issue of tithing. The practical implications of the New Testament principle of total disposition renders the tithe obsolete, unless it is used as an aid to help Christians discover in greater fullness the joy of worship through giving.

For Christians whose limited income is only sufficient for subsistence, the tithe provides a goal to attain.

For more affluent Christians whose income exceeds their needs, the tithe becomes restrictive. It is to be surpassed in the same measure that God prospers them.

To insure the proper functioning of the ministries of the local church, it is appropriate for a body of believers to require that, apart from other giving, at least a tenth of their members' income be contributed to the local church that serves them. Both Old and New Testament offer warrant to uphold such a standard (Leviticus 27:30-32; Matthew 23:23).

Motives Matter

Purpose

One day, while looking through the newspaper, you spot an ad: OFFICE MANAGER WANTED. NO EXPERIENCE NECESSARY. GENEROUS SALARY AND BENEFITS. CALL 555-3331. You've been restless lately, hoping for a new challenge, so you decide to answer the ad. Surprisingly, you discover over the phone that no one else has responded to the notice. You go in for an interview and talk to a gruff old man who tells you you'll be working for him. You're not sure you like him, but everything else seems satisfying.

A few weeks into the job, you're unhappy. The work is repetitive and not too challenging, and the old man, while not rude, doesn't talk very much to you. You don't feel motivated to put in a full day's work, and you start cutting corners and taking longer breaks. But one day while your employer is away, you stumble across a file that contains some startling information. You find out that your boss is a multi-millionaire. Moreover, you uncover a will that contains the names of past office managers—all of whom are slated to receive several hundred thousand dollars.

Overnight, you become the model employee. Your enthusiasm improves markedly, and your employer, noticing the change, compliments you on your renewed dedication. But you begin to hear in your mind nagging questions: *Am I just changing my behavior so I can get some reward? What are my motives for staying with this job? Am I being a hypocrite, only pretending to care about my boss's well-being when I really want his money?*

Christians should always subject their motives for serving others to the same kind of scrutiny. Jesus thought that this was so important that he talked about it at length in the Sermon on the Mount. During this study, we will examine Matthew 6:1-18 as we try to sort out the importance of motives in our service to God and others.

Study

Why did Jesus criticize the Pharisees even though they were performing acts of charity?

Why would Jesus say that a person who had publicly announced his deeds had received his reward in full? (Matthew 6:2, 5, 16)

Why would motives matter so much to God–isn't it sufficient to "get the good deed done" without examining motives?

Why did Jesus tell us that when we give, the left hand should not know what the right hand is doing?

What do you think causes people to have mixed motives when they serve?

What tempts you to serve with mixed motives?

How can we have improper motives when we pray? (Matthew 6:7-8)

Why did the hypocrites draw attention to their fasting? (Matthew 6:16-17)

What makes it hard for you to serve in secret?

What do you think are the rewards that God provides?

What is your response to this passage with regard to application?

BOTTOM LINE

Bible

Read Revelation 2:1-29, noting observations and applications.

Prayer

Day One: Examine your motives for giving to others. Pray that you would give in such a way that "your left hand would not know what your right hand is doing."

Day Two: In what ways have you prayed so as to impress others? When have you just uttered words instead of engaging your heart in prayer? Ask God to cleanse your prayer life of these problems.

Day Three: How would your spiritual life be improved by periodically taking up a discipline like fasting? Prayerfully consider doing so, keeping in mind the manner in which we should practice fasting (Matthew 6:16-18).

Scripture Memory

Be careful not to do your "acts of righteousness" before men, to be seen by them. If you do, you will have no reward from your Father in heaven. Matthew 6:1

The next study will be the first two of two concerning the seven churches described in Revelation 2:1–3:22. To prepare, ask yourself: What strengths and problems does my church have? If Jesus were to return today, what would he find to praise or criticize in my fellowship?

Lessons from Seven Churches (Part 1)

PURPOSE

Ephesus, Smyrna, Pergamum, and Thyatira. Are these exotic spices for a secret recipe? Or perhaps the latest in fashion colors?

In the Book of Revelation, the Apostle John was instructed by Christ to convey messages to seven churches. These churches often had both considerable strengths and very serious shortcomings. Like our churches today, they struggled with losing their love for Christ and slipping into immorality, leniency, compromise, lifelessness, or casualness about their faith. The encouragement and warning that Christ gives these Christians is timeless, and all believers should heed these words as relevant to their own situations.

In this study, we will study the messages given to the churches at Ephesus, Smyrna, Pergamum, and Thyatira. Pay attention especially to the message to Ephesus, for its words of warning are applicable to many contemporary churches today.

STUDY

Ephesus

Ephesus was the capital of Asia Minor, a center of land and sea trade, and, along with Alexandria and Antioch in Syria, one of the three most influential cities in the eastern part of the Roman empire. The temple of Artemis, one of the ancient wonders of the world, was located in this city, and a major industry was the manufacture of images of this goddess (see Acts 19:21-41).

Over a long period of time, the church had steadfastly refused to tolerate sin among its members. This was not easy in a city noted for immoral sexual practices associated with the worship of the goddess Artemis. But many of the second-generation believers had lost their zeal for God. They were a busy church—the members did much to benefit themselves and the community—but they were acting out of the wrong motives. (From the *Life Application Bible,* NIV)

What commendable characteristics did the church of Ephesus have? (Revelation 2:1-3)

How is your church commendable like the Ephesian church?

How had the Ephesian church fallen? (Revelation 2:4-5)

What did Jesus urge the Ephesians to do?

What promises did Jesus offer for those who "overcome"? (Revelation 2:7)

If your pastor called you and asked for your advice on how to get your church to grow more devoted to Christ, what would you suggest?

Smyrna

The city of Smyrna was about 25 miles north of Ephesus. It was nicknamed "Port of Asia" because it had an excellent harbor on the Aegean Sea. The church in this city struggled against two hostile forces: a Jewish population strongly opposed to Christianity, and a non-Jewish population that was loyal to Rome and supported emperor worship. Persecution and suffering were inevitable in an environment like this. (From the *Life Application Bible,* NIV)

Why were the believers in Smyrna "rich"? (Revelation 2:9)

What were these believers about to suffer? (Revelation 2:10)

What reward was promised to those who withstood these trials? (Revelation 2:10-11)

How would Jesus' words to this church be relevant to the situation your church is going through?

Pergamum

The city of Pergamum was built on a hill 1,000 feet above the surrounding countryside, creating a natural fortress. It was a sophisticated city, a center of Greek culture and education, with a 200,000 volume library. But it was also the center of four cults and it rivaled Ephesus in its worship of idols. The city's chief god was Asclepius, whose symbol was a serpent, and who was considered the god of healing. It was not easy to be a Christian in Pergamum. Believers experienced great pressure to compromise or leave the faith. (From the *Life Application Bible,* NIV)

Why were the believers in Pergamum praised for their faith? (Revelation 2:12-13)

What did Christ hold against the church of Pergamum? (Revelation 2:14-17)

In what ways might these ancient problems in Pergamum surface in your church?

Thyatira

Thyatira was a working man's town, with many trade guilds for cloth making, dyeing, and pottery. The city was basically secular, with no focus on any particular religion. (From the *Life Application Bible,* NIV)

What grievous sin had the church of Thyatira tolerated? (Revelation 2:20-22)

What promise did Jesus hold out to those believers who had not stumbled? (Revelation 2:24-28)

Conclusion

Which of the four messages studied in this lesson would be most relevant to your church? Why?

Bottom line

Your walk with God

Bible

Read and study Revelation 3:1-22.

Prayer

Day One: Pray that your church would not lose its first love and that its work for the Kingdom would be profitable.

Day Two: Pray that your church would keep itself from false teaching and immoral practices.

Day Three: Pray that your church would be ready for adversity and even persecution by standing up for Christ.

Scripture Memory

Through Jesus, therefore, let us continually offer to God a sacrifice of praise–the fruit of lips that confess his name. And do not forget to do good and to share with others, for with such sacrifices God is pleased. Hebrews 13:15-16

The next study will conclude the discussion of the seven churches. To prepare, ask yourself: In what way, if any, is my participation in the life of the church lukewarm?

12

Lessons from Seven Churches (Part 2)

Purpose

It is a sweltering hot summer day. You've just come in from painting your house, and you've in need of a refreshing drink. Your friend promises to bring you "just the thing" if you'll wait by the back door. When he arrives a few moments later, you take the glass from his hands, take a big gulp, . . . and gag. You realize that you are drinking a tall glass of lukewarm tea!

Or imagine a similar scene in the same house six months later. You've just dug your car out of a huge snow drift. The wind chill is forty below zero, and you're chilled to the bone.

You could use a hot cup of coffee and a warm blanket right away. Another friend standing in the kitchen volunteers to help you out. She hands you an afghan and that eagerly anticipated cup of coffee. You take a big swallow from the cup . . . and wince. The coffee is lukewarm!

Our disgust with lukewarm refreshments is similar to the distaste Jesus showed for the church of Laodicea, the last of the seven congregations he spoke to in Revelation 2:1–3:22. Laodicea had become lukewarm in its fervor for Christ and was ignorant of its spiritual poverty. It shared similarities with church at Sardis, which once had once possessed a reputation for fruitfulness but then slipped into decay. For these churches, as for our churches today, the only cure for their spiritual sickness would come through faithful obedience to Christ.

STUDY

Sardis

The wealthy city of Sardis was actually in two locations. The older section of the city was on a mountain, and when its population outgrew the spot, a newer section was built on the city below. The problem in the Sardis church was not heresy, but spiritual death. In spite of its reputation for being active, Sardis was infested with sin. Its deeds were evil and its clothes were soiled. (From the *Life Application Bible,* NIV)

What kind of a reputation did the church of Sardis have? (Revelation 3:1)

What did Christ urge the church of Sardis to do? (Revelation 3:2-3)

What kind of a reputation does your church have?

What might Jesus say about the spiritual life of your church?

Philadelphia

Philadelphia was founded by the citizens of Pergamum. The community was built in a frontier area as a gateway to the central plateau of Asia Minor. Philadelphia's residents kept barbarians out of the region and brought in Greek culture and language. The city was destroyed by an earthquake in A.D. 17, and aftershocks kept the people so worried that most of them lived outside the city limits. (From the *Life Application Bible,* NIV)

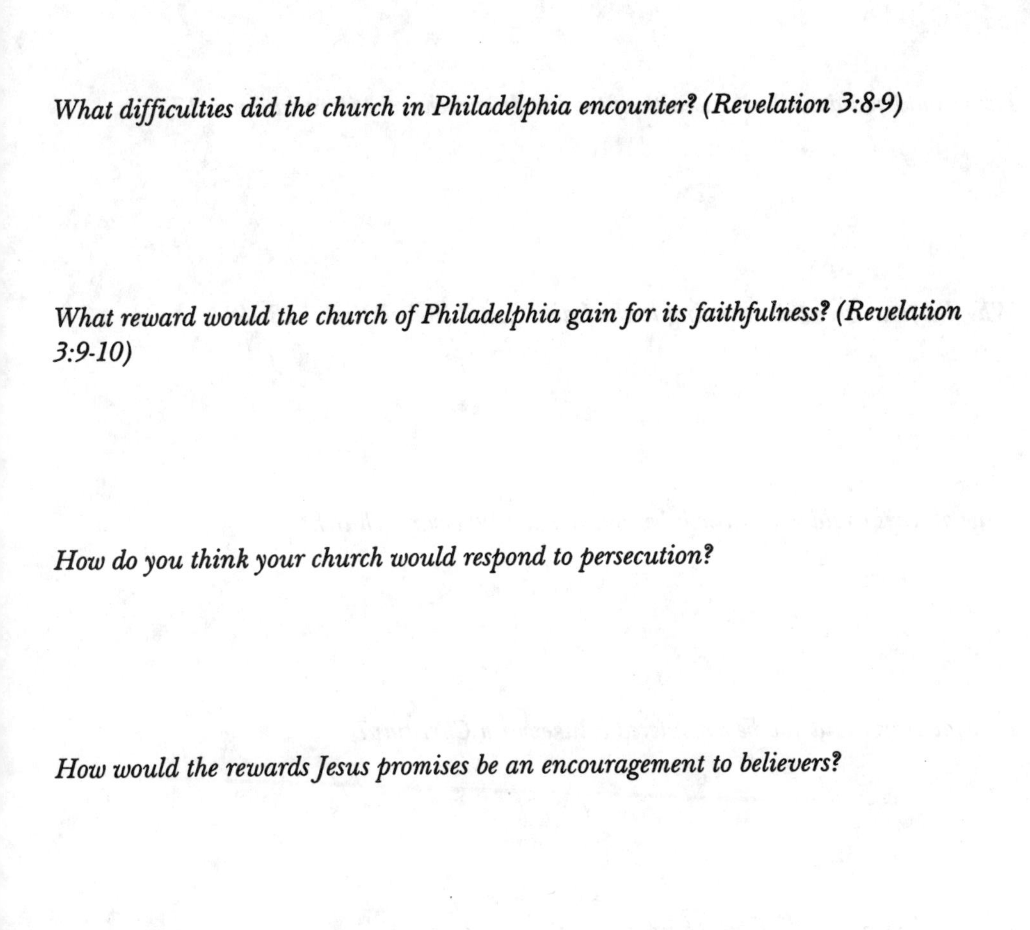

What difficulties did the church in Philadelphia encounter? (Revelation 3:8-9)

What reward would the church of Philadelphia gain for its faithfulness? (Revelation 3:9-10)

How do you think your church would respond to persecution?

How would the rewards Jesus promises be an encouragement to believers?

Laodicea

Laodicea was the wealthiest of the seven cities, known for its banking industry, manufacture of wool, and a medical school that produced an eye salve. But the city always had a problem with its water supply. At one time an aqueduct was built to bring water to the city from hot springs. But by the time the water reached the city, it was neither hot nor refreshingly cool–only lukewarm. The church had become as bland as the tepid water that came into the city. (From the *Life Application Bible,* NIV)

What does it mean that the deeds of the Laodiceans were neither cold nor hot? (Revelation 3:16)

How would you describe the wealth of the Laodicean church? (Revelation 3:17)

Why did Jesus give this warning to the Laodiceans? (Revelation 3:18-19)

In what ways could your church be considered a lukewarm church?

In what ways could you be considered a lukewarm Christian?

How can a lukewarm spiritual life be made warm hot?

How can a lukewarm church be made hot?

Bottom Line

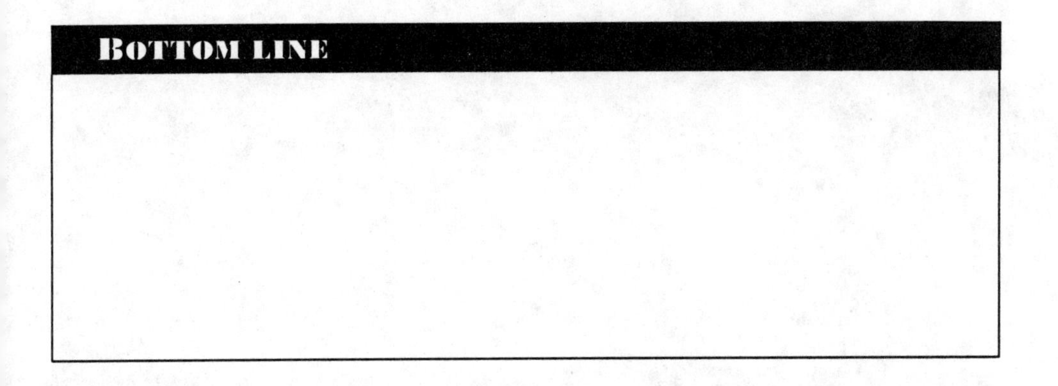

Your Walk with God

Bible

Reread Philippians 2:1-30 this week, and reflect on how your attitude toward service has changed.

Prayer

On each of three days, pray for a different member of your group. Ask God to help them put into practice the lessons conveyed in this study guide.

Scripture Memory

Review 2 Corinthians 9:7, Matthew 6:1, and Hebrews 13:15-16 for next week.

The final session of *Building Your Church* will be a review of the material covered in the first twelve sessions.

Reviewing Building Your Church

PURPOSE

Training camp is over! It's time for the season to begin. You've spent twelve weeks learning, praying about, and studying God's instructions for service. Now you've been placed in the starting lineup, and you will need to draw on all the resources you have available to you to put forth the best effort for God's team. He's called you, equipped you, and empowered you to carry out his will and build his church.

Let's get our final instruction and then PLAY BALL!

STUDY

What mistaken attitudes can we have in our service to God?

What prevents the church from exercising its spiritual gifts in an efficient, harmonious manner?

What are your primary spiritual gifts? In what ways can you gifts be best utilized to build your church?

Why are the complementary gifts to be used only to supplement the primary gifts?

If you were to try to convince a brand new believer of the importance of discovering and using his spiritual gifts, what would you tell him?

How would you summarize Jesus' teaching on money and possessions?

If you were asked by that same new believer to explain how God wants him to handle his money, including giving to ministry, what would you tell him? Write down at least three suggestions.

How will you handle your own resources differently as a result of this study? Be specific.

What passages of Scripture in this study have helped you rethink your attitudes toward possessions?

What principle should believers keep in mind when they're determining how much to give to their church or other ministries?

Looking back at the messages given to each of the seven churches in Revelation 2 and 3, what related problems in your own church could weaken its effectiveness?

What step could you take as an individual in response to Jesus' message to the seven churches?

BOTTOM LINE

YOUR WALK WITH GOD

Bible

Choose any passage of Scripture for next time, noting observations and applications.

Prayer

During your three sessions of prayer, include elements of the following: adoration, confession, thanksgiving, supplication.

Scripture Memory

Review 1 Corinthians 14:1, Ephesians 6:7, 1 Corinthians 12:7, 1 Peter 4:10, Luke 16:11, Hebrews 13:5, 2 Corinthians 9:7, Matthew 6:1, and Hebrews 13:15-16.

ON YOUR OWN

Self-Evaluation

Your group leader will be meeting with you to discuss your current spiritual condition and your hopes for growing in your faith. Please take some time to reflect honestly on where you stand right now within these four basic categories of Christian growth. Rate yourself in each category.

+ **Doing well. I'm pleased with my progress so far.**

✓ **On the right track, but I see definite areas for improvement.**

– **This is a struggle. I need some help.**

A Disciple Is One Who . . .

Walks with God

To what extent is my Bible study and prayer time adequate for helping me walk with God?

Rating:

Comments:

Lives the Word

To what extent is my mind filled with scriptural truths so that my actions and reactions show I am being transformed?

Rating:

Comments:

Contributes to the work

To what extent am I actively participating in the church with my time, talents, and treasures?

Rating:

Comments:

Impacts the world

To what extent am I impacting my world with a Christian witness and influence?

Rating:

Comments:

Other issues I would like to discuss with my small group leader:

The *Walking With God Journal* is the perfect companion to the *Walking With God Series.* Use it to keep your notes during Bible study, record your prayers, or simply jot down your thoughts and insights. (0-310-91642-9)

NOTES

NOTES

NOTES

NOTES

NOTES